Super Mario Crochet Design

Adorable Mario Pattern For Your Weekend

Copyright © 2021

All rights reserved.

DEDICATION

The author and publisher have provided this e-book to you for your personal use only. You may not make this e-book publicly available in any way. Copyright infringement is against the law. If you believe the copy of this e-book you are reading infringes on the author's copyright, please notify the publisher at: https://us.macmillan.com/piracy

Contents

Mini Green Gamer Friend 1

Mini Red Gamer Friend 17

Mini Birdo Gamer Friend 33

Mini Yoshi Gamer Friend 54

Koopa Troopa Pattern 74

Mario Bros. Cheep-Cheep 83

Mini Green Gamer Friend

Supplies

- Worsted weight [4] yarn in colors listed.
- Brown (Shoes, Sideburns) Red Heart: Café Latte [20 yards]
- Blue (Pants) Red Heart: Royal [50 yards]
- Green (Shirt, Hat) Red Heart Cherry Red [20 yards]
- Lt Peach (Skin) Hobby Lobby I Love This Yarn: Light Peach [40 yards]
- Black (Moustache) Red Heart: Black [5 yards]
- White (Beard, Eyes) Red Heart: White [5 yards]
- Yellow (Buttons) Red Heart: Yellow [scrap]
- Crochet hook size F/5 (3.75mm)
- 9mm Plastic Safety Eyes
- Yarn needle

- Stitch markers
- Fiberfill or stuffing of choice.

Finished doll is about 5" tall if using worsted weight yarn.

Abbreviations

- ch - chain
- sc – single crochet
- hdc – half double crochet
- dc – double crochet
- tc – treble crochet
- dec – decrease (stitch next 2 stitches together)
- inc – increase (stitch 2 times into the next stitch)
- sl st – slip stitch
- st(s) – stitch(es)
- sk – skip chain or stitch
- sp – space

- lp st – loop stitch (youtube has some excellent tutorials if you don't know how to do this stitch)
- BLO – back loop only
- FLO – front loop only
- R – round
- [ ] repeat work as directed
- ( ) number of stitches you should have at the end of your round
- FO - finish off
- MR – magic ring

Super Mario Crochet Design

Before you begin:

- This amigurumi/plush is worked in continuous rounds. Mark the beginning of each round with a stitch marker.

- Use the "magic ring" when starting rounds, there are many youtube videos teaching how to make a magic ring or magic circle. An alternative method to the magic ring is: ch2, sc x6 (or number of sts noted) in 2nd ch from hook, sl st to join. Continue on in rounds as noted above.
- Gauge is not important in this project as long as you are consistent with your tension.
- This project is made with all sc stitches unless otherwise specified.
- TIP: Always change colors in the stitch BEFORE the color change by pulling the new color through the 2 loops, thus beginning with the correct

color on your hook!

Shoes/Legs – make 2

With brown

R1: MR 6

R2: inc x6 (12)

R3: [inc, sc 1] x6 (18)

R4: sc 4, dec x5, sc 4 (13)

R5: sc 6, dec, sc 5 (12)

Change to blue.

R6: BLO sc 12

R7-8: sc 12

FO, hide tail.

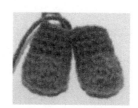

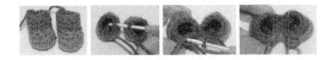

Body/Head

With blue

R1: Pick up both legs, face feet so they are pointing in the same direction and

away from you. Insert hook in middle stitches and sc legs together. The middle

joining sc will not count in your stitch count. The next stitch you make will be

in the leg on your left and this will be the beginning stitch so place your stitch

marker here. Continue around left leg and then go around right leg. You want

to be working from the back so your color changes don't show. (22)

R2: [inc, sc 3] x5, sc 2 (27)

R3-4: sc 27

R5: [dec, sc 7] x3 (24)

Change to green.

R6: BLO sc 24

R7: [dec, sc 2] x6 (18)

R8: [dec, sc 1] x6 (12)

Change to skin color

R9: inc x12 (24)

R10: [inc, sc 2] x8 (32)

R11-17: sc 32

R18: [dec, sc 2] x8 (24)

Stuff legs and body firmly.

Insert 9mm eyes between R15-R16, 3 sts apart.

R19: [dec, sc 1] x8 (16)

Stuff head firmly.

R20: dec x8 (8)

Finish stuffing.

R21: dec x3

FO, hide tail.

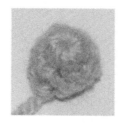

Nose

With skin color

R1: MR 6

R2-3: sc 6

FO, leave tail for sewing to face.

Sew to face.

Moustache

With black

Ch 8 (this is your base chain), sl st in 2nd ch from hook, hdc, dc, sl st, dc,

hdc, sl st

FO, leave tail for sewing to face.

Sew to face just under nose

Hat

With green

R1: MR 6

R2: inc x6 (12)

R3: [inc, sc 1] x6 (18)

R4: [sc 2, inc] x6 (24)

R5: [inc, sc 3] x6 (30)

R6: sc 2, [inc, sc 4] x5, inc, sc 2 (36)

R7: [sc 5, inc] x6 (42)

R8: sc 42

R9: [dec, sc 2] x10, dec (31)

R10: [dec, sc 2] x6, BLO sc 7 (25)

The next 2 rows are the brim and are worked flat, not in the round.

R11-12: ch 1, turn, sc 7

FO, leave tail for sewing to head.

Sew to head. Attach hat to head using a running stitch one stitch up from the

bottom of the hat. That way a small lip is left to slip the top of the sideburns

and hair under.

Ears – make 2

With skin color

MR 6, do not join in circle.

FO, leave tail for sewing to face.

Sew to face.

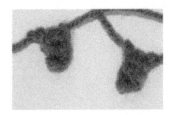

Sideburns – make 2

With brown

Ch 4, turn, sc in 2nd ch from hook, sc 2 (3)

FO, leave tail for sewing to face.

Slip under hat lip and sew to face in front of ears.

Hair

With brown

Ch 17, sl st in 3rd ch from hook, [ch 2, sk next st, sl st in next st] x7

FO, leave tail for sewing to head.

Slip under hat lip and sew to head.

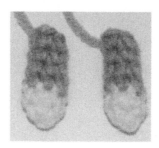

Arms – make 2

With white

R1: MR 6

R2: sc 6

Change to green

R3-6: sc 6

FO, leave tail for sewing to body.

Sew to sides of body.

No need to stuff arms.

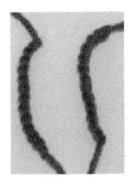

Suspenders – make 2

With blue

Begin with long tail, ch 12

FO, leave tail for sewing to body.

Sew to body at front and back pants.

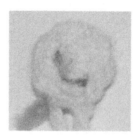

"L" Spot

With white

MR 6

Join & FO, leave tail for sewing to body.

Embroider "L" on spot with green.

Sew spot to center of hat front.

Use black yarn to embroider eyebrows.

With yellow yarn make a French knot or embroider a button on the bottom front of the 2 suspenders.

Mini Red Gamer Friend

Supplies
- Worsted weight [4] yarn in colors listed.

- Brown (Shoes, Sideburns) Red Heart: Café Latte [20 yards]
- Blue (Pants) Red Heart: Royal [80 yards]
- Red (Shirt, Hat) Red Heart Cherry Red [20 yards]
- Lt Peach (Skin) Hobby Lobby I Love This Yarn: Light Peach [50 yards]
- Black (Moustache) Red Heart: Black [5 yards]
- White (Beard, Eyes) Red Heart: White [5 yards]
- Yellow (Buttons) Red Heart: Yellow [scrap]
- Crochet hook size F/5 (3.75mm)
- 9mm Plastic Safety Eyes
- Yarn needle
- Stitch markers
- Fiberfill or stuffing of choice.

Finished doll is about 5" tall if using worsted weight yarn.

Abbreviations

ch - chain

- sc – single crochet
- hdc – half double crochet
- dc – double crochet
- tc – treble crochet
- dec – decrease (stitch next 2 stitches together)
- inc – increase (stitch 2 times into the next stitch)
- sl st – slip stitch
- st(s) – stitch(es)
- sk – skip chain or stitch
- sp – space
- lp st – loop stitch (youtube has some excellent tutorials if you don't know

how to do this stitch)

- BLO – back loop only

- FLO – front loop only
- R – round
- [ ] repeat work as directed
- ( ) number of stitches you should have at the end of your round
- FO - finish off
- MR – magic ring

Before you begin:

- This amigurumi/plush is worked in continuous rounds. Mark the beginning
- of each round with a stitch marker.
- Use the "magic ring" when starting rounds, there are many youtube

videos teaching how to make a magic ring or magic circle. An alternative

method to the magic ring is: ch2, sc x6 (or number of sts noted) in 2nd

ch from hook, sl st to join. Continue on in rounds as noted above.

- Gauge is not important in this project as long as you are consistent with
- your tension.
- This project is made with all sc stitches unless otherwise specified.

- TIP: Always change colors in the stitch BEFORE the color change by pulling the new color through the 2 loops, thus beginning with the correct color on your hook!

Shoes/Legs – make 2

With brown

R1: MR 6

R2: inc x6 (12)

R3: [inc, sc 1] x6 (18)

R4: sc 4, dec x5, sc 4 (13)

R5: sc 6, dec, sc 5 (12)

Change to blue

R6: BLO sc 12

R7-8: sc 12

FO, hide tail.

Body/Head

With blue

R1: Pick up both legs, face feet so they are pointing in the same direction and
away from you. Insert hook in middle stitches and sc legs together. The middle
joining sc will not count in your stitch count. The next stitch you make will be
in the leg on your left and this will be the beginning stitch so place your stitch
marker here. Continue around left leg and then go around right leg. You want
to be working from the back so your color changes don't show. (22)

R2: [inc, sc 3] x5, sc 2 (27)

R3-4: sc 27

R5: [dec, sc 7] x3 (24)

Change to red.

R6: BLO sc 24

R7: [dec, sc 2] x6 (18)

R8: [dec, sc 1] x6 (12)

Change to skin color.

R9: inc x12 (24)

R10: [inc, sc 1] x12 (36)

R11-17: sc 36

R18: [dec, sc 1] x12 (24)

Stuff legs and body firmly.

Insert 9mm eyes between R15-R16, 3 sts apart.

R19: [dec, sc 1] x8 (16)

Stuff head firmly.

R20: dec x8 (8)

Finish stuffing.

R21: dec x3

FO, hide tail.

Nose

With skin color

R1: MR 6

R2-3: sc 6

FO, leave tail for sewing to face.

Sew to face.

Moustache

With black

Ch 8 (this is your base chain), sl st in 3rd ch from hook

[ch 2, sl st in next base chain stitch] x5

FO, leave tail for sewing to face.

Sew to face just under nose.

Hat

With red

R1: MR 6

R2: inc x6 (12)

R3: [inc, sc 1] x6 (18)

R4: [sc 2, inc] x6 (24)

R5: [inc, sc 3] x6 (30)

R6: sc 2, [inc, sc 4] x5, inc, sc 2 (36)

R7: [sc 5, inc] x6 (42)

R8: sc 42

R9: [dec, sc 2] x10, dec (31)

R10: [dec, sc 2] x6, BLO sc 7 (25)

The next 2 rows are the brim and are worked flat, not in the round.

R11-12: ch 1, turn, sc 7

FO, leave tail for sewing to head.

Sew to head. Attach hat to head using a running stitch one stitch up from the

bottom of the hat. That way a small lip is left to slip the top of the sideburns

and hair under.

Ears – make 2

With skin color

MR 6, do not join in circle.

FO, leave tail for sewing to face.

Sew to face.

Sideburns – make 2

With brown

Ch 4, turn, sc in 2nd ch from hook, sc 2 (3)

FO, leave tail for sewing to face.

Slip under hat lip and sew to face in front of ears.

Hair

With brown

Ch 17, sl st in 3rd ch from hook, [ch 2, sk next st, sl st in next st] x7

FO, leave tail for sewing to head.

Slip under hat lip and sew to head.

Arms – make 2

With white

R1: MR 6

R2: sc 6

Change to red

R3-6: sc 6

FO, leave tail for sewing to body.

Sew to sides of body.

No need to stuff arms.

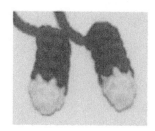

Suspenders – make 2

With blue

Begin with long tail, ch 12

FO, leave tail for sewing to body.

Sew to body at front and back pants.

"M" Spot

With white

MR 6

Join & FO, leave tail for sewing to body.

Embroider "M" on spot with red.

Sew spot to center of hat front.

Use black yarn to embroider eyebrows.

With yellow yarn make a French knot or embroider a button on the bottom
front of the 2 suspenders

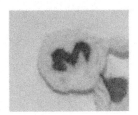

Super Mario Crochet Design

Mini Birdo Gamer Friend

Supplies

- Worsted weight [4] yarn in colors listed.
- MC (Body, Arms, Nose, Tail, Legs) [80 yards]
- White (Eyes, Belly) [30 yards]
- Red (Bow, Spikes) [20 yards]
- Black (Nose, Eyelashes) [10 yds]
- CC1 (Face Spots) [scrap]
- Crochet hook size F/5 (3.75mm)
- 9mm Plastic Safety Eyes
- Yarn needle
- Stitch markers
- Fiberfill or stuffing of choice.

Finished doll is about 5" tall if using worsted weight yarn.

Abbreviations

- ch - chain
- sc – single crochet
- hdc – half double crochet
- dc – double crochet
- tc – treble crochet
- dec – decrease (stitch next 2 stitches together)
- inc – increase (stitch 2 times into the next stitch)
- sl st – slip stitch
- st(s) – stitch(es)
- sk – skip chain or stitch
- sp – space
- lp st – loop stitch (youtube has some excellent tutorials if you don't know how to do this stitch)
- BLO – back loop only

Super Mario Crochet Design

- FLO – front loop only
- R – round
- [ ] repeat work as directed
- ( ) number of stitches you should have at the end of your round
- FO - finish off
- MR – magic ring

Before you begin:

- This amigurumi/plush is worked in continuous rounds. Mark the beginning
- of each round with a stitch marker.
- Use the "magic ring" when starting rounds, there are many youtube

videos teaching how to make a magic ring or magic circle. An alternative

method to the magic ring is: ch2, sc x6 (or number of sts noted) in 2nd

ch from hook, sl st to join. Continue on in rounds as noted above.

- Gauge is not important in this project as long as you are consistent with
- your tension.
- This project is made with all sc stitches unless otherwise specified.

- TIP: Always change colors in the stitch BEFORE the color change by pulling the new color through the 2 loops, thus beginning with the correct color on your hook!

Body/Head

With MC

R1: MR 6

R2: inc x6 (12)

R3: [inc, sc 1] x6 (18)

R4: [inc, sc 2] x6 (24)

R5: [inc, sc 3] x6 (30)

R6-9: sc 30

R10: [dec, sc 4] x5 (25)

R11: sc 25

R12: [dec, sc 3] x5 (20)

R13: sc 20

R14: [dec, sc 2] x5 (15)

R15: [dec, sc 3] x3 (12)

R16: inc x12 (24)

R17: sc 4, [inc, sc 1] x2, sc 6, [sc 1, inc] x2, sc 6 (28)

R18-20: sc 28

R21: sc 4, [dec, sc 1] x2, sc 6, [sc 1, dec] x2, sc 6 (24)

R22: sc 3, [dec, sc 1] x2, sc 5, [dec, sc 1] x2, sc 4 (20)

R23: [dec, sc 2] x5 (15)

R24-27: sc 15

Stuff firmly.

FO, leave tail and use it to sew hole closed

Eyes

With white

Eyes are worked flat

R1: ch 7, turn, sc in 2nd ch from hook, sc 5 (6)

R2-3: ch 1, turn, sc 6

R4: turn, sk 1st st, dc, sl st x2, dc, sl st

Sl st around entire eyes

FO, leave tail for sewing to head.

Insert 9mm eyes. Put back on eyes and push stem through Birdo's head.

Sew to head.

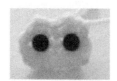

Eyelids

With MC

R1: ch 10, sc in 2nd ch from hook, sc 8 (9)

R2: sc 9

FO, leave tail for sewing to eyes.

Sew to eyes.

With black, make eyelashes and line between eyelids and eyes.

Belly

With white

Belly is worked flat.

R1: ch 6, turn, sc in 2nd ch from hook, sc 4 (5)

R2: ch 1, turn, inc, sc 3, inc (7)

R3: ch 1, turn, sc 7

R4: ch 1, turn, inc, sc 5, inc (9)

R5-7: ch 1, turn, sc 9

R8: ch 1, turn, dec, sc 5, dec (7)

R9: ch 1, turn, dec, sc 3, dec (5)

R10: ch 1, turn, dec, sc 1, dec (3)

Sc around entire belly.

FO, leave tail for sewing to body.

Sew to front of body.

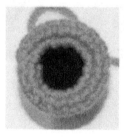 

Nose

With Black

R1: MR 6

R2: inc x6 (12)

Change to MC.

R3: FLO [inc, sc 1] x6 (18)

R4: FLO sc 18

R5: sc 18

R6: sc 18 with back loops from R4

R7: [dec, sc 1] x6 (12)

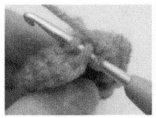 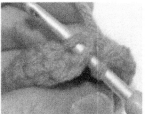

R8-10: sc 12

R11: [inc, sc 1] x6 (18)

FO, leave tail for sewing to face.

Stuff lightly.

Sew to face.

With CC1, embroider spots on cheeks.

Tail

With MC

R1: MR 4

R2: [inc, sc 1] x2 (6)

R3: [inc, sc 2] x2 (8)

R4: [inc, sc 3] x2 (10)

R5: sc 2, inc, sc 4, inc, sc 2 (12)

R6: inc, hdc 5, inc, sc 5 (14)

R7: inc, hdc 6, inc, sc 6 (16)

R8: inc, hdc 7, inc, sc 7 (18)

FO, leave tail for sewing to body.

Stuff.

Sew to body.

Bow

With red

R1: ch 11, sc in 2nd ch from hook, sc 8, 2 sc in next st, continue around other side of ch. Sc 9 (20)

R2-3: sc 20

R4: [dec, sc 3] x4 (16)

R5: [dec, sc 2] x4 (12)

R6: sc 12

R7: [dec, sc 1] x4 (8)

R8: inc x8 (16)

R9-10: sc 16

R11: dec x8 (8)

R12: [inc, sc 1] x4 (12)

R13: sc 12

R14: [inc, sc 2] x4 (16)

R15: [inc, sc 3] x4 (20)

R16-18: sc 20

FO, leave tail for sewing closed.

Stuff lightly.

Sew opening closed

Wrap yarn around each side of "knot" section.

Sew to back of head.

Arms – make 2

With MC

R1: MR 6

R2-8: sc 6

FO, leave tail for sewing to body.

Sew to sides of body.

No need to stuff arms.

Legs – make 2

With MC

R1: MR 6

R2: [inc, sc 1] x3 (9)

R3: [inc, sc 2] x3 (12)

R4: [inc, sc 3] x3 (15)

R5: sc 15

FO, leave tail for sewing to body.

Stuff lightly.

Sew to body.

Foot – make 2

With white

R1: MR 6

R2: inc x6 (12)

Change to MC

R3: [inc, sc 1] x6 (18)

R4: BLO sc 18

R5: sc 6, dec x3, sc 6 (15)

R6: sc 5, dec x3, sc 4 (12)

R7: sc 12

FO, leave tail for sewing to body.

With white, embroider 3 claws on each foot.

Stuff

Sew to body. Feet can be placed so they make Birdo stand or sit.

Back Spikes

With red

This is all worked as one long piece without cutting. I have labeled it S (for spike) for ease of keeping track of where you are.

S1: ch 4, turn, sl st in 2nd ch from hook, sc, hdc

S2-5: [ch 6, sl st, sc, hdc, dc, tc] x4

S6: ch 4, turn, sl st in 2nd ch from hook, sc, hdc

FO, leave tail

Fold in half and sew spikes together. This makes them firm so they won't curl.

Sew to back of body.

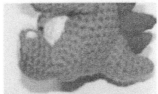

Congratulations!

Your Mini Gamer Friend is now complete and ready for play or display. I hope
you enjoyed making this pattern. I would love to see pictures of your finished
dolls!!

Note: Be careful when giving your finished plush to young ones. Your amigurumi
now contains small parts and pieces. If these pieces were to come off, they
could pose a choking hazard to small children and pets.

Super Mario Crochet Design

Mini Yoshi Gamer Friend

Supplies

- Worsted weight [4] yarn in colors listed.
- MC (Body, Arms, Nose, Tail, Legs) [100 yards]
- White (Eyes, Belly) [30 yards]
- Red (Shell, Spikes) [20 yards]
- CC1 (Shoe Sole) [10 yards]
- CC2 (Shoe) [20 yards]
- Crochet hook size F/5 (3.75mm)
- 9mm Plastic Safety Eyes
- Yarn needle
- Stitch markers
- Fiberfill or stuffing of choice.

Finished doll is about 5" tall if using worsted weight yarn.

Abbreviations

- ch - chain

- sc – single crochet
- hdc – half double crochet
- dc – double crochet
- tc – treble crochet
- dec – decrease (stitch next 2 stitches together)
- inc – increase (stitch 2 times into the next stitch)
- sl st – slip stitch
- st(s) – stitch(es)
- sk – skip chain or stitch
- sp – space
- lp st – loop stitch (youtube has some excellent tutorials if you don't know how to do this stitch)
- BLO – back loop only
- FLO – front loop only
- R – round

- [ ] repeat work as directed
- ( ) number of stitches you should have at the end of your round
- FO - finish off
- MR – magic ring

Before you begin:

- This amigurumi/plush is worked in continuous rounds. Mark the beginning

of each round with a stitch marker.
- Use the "magic ring" when starting rounds, there are many youtube videos teaching how to make a magic ring or magic circle. An alternative method to the magic ring is: ch2, sc x6 (or number of sts noted) in 2nd ch from hook, sl st to join. Continue on in rounds as noted above.
- Gauge is not important in this project as long as you are consistent with your tension.
- This project is made with all sc stitches unless otherwise specified.
- TIP: Always change colors in the stitch BEFORE the color change by pulling the new color through the 2 loops, thus beginning with the correct color on your hook!

Body/Head

With MC

R1: MR 6

R2: inc x6 (12)

R3: [inc, sc 1] x6 (18)

R4: [inc, sc 2] x6 (24)

R5: [inc, sc 3] x6 (30)

R6-9: sc 30

R10: [dec, sc 4] x5 (25)

R11: sc 25

R12: [dec, sc 3] x5 (20)

R13: sc 20

R14: [dec, sc 2] x5 (15)

R15: [dec, sc 3] x3 (12)

R16: inc x12 (24)

R17: sc 4, [inc, sc 1] x2, sc 6, [sc 1, inc] x2, sc 6 (28)

R18-20: sc 28

R21: sc 4, [dec, sc 1] x2, sc 6, [sc 1, dec] x2, sc 6 (24)

R22: sc 3, [dec, sc 1] x2, sc 5, [dec, sc 1] x2, sc 4 (20)

R23: [dec, sc 2] x5 (15)

R24-25: sc 15

R26: [dec, sc 1] x5 (10)

R27: sc 10

Stuff firmly.

FO, leave tail and use it to sew hole closed.

Eyes

With white

Eyes are worked flat

R1: ch 7, turn, sc in 2nd ch from hook, sc 5 (6)

R2-3: ch 1, turn, sc 6

R4: turn, sk 1st st, dc, sl st x2, dc, sl st

Sl st around entire eyes

FO, leave tail for sewing to head.

Insert 9mm eyes. Put back on eyes and push stem through Yoshi's head.

Sew to head.

Cheeks – make 2

With white

R1: MR 6

R2: [inc, sc 1] x3 (9)

R3: [inc, sc 2] x3 (12)

R4: [inc, sc 3] x3 (15)

FO, leave tail for sewing to head.

Lightly stuff

Sew to head.

Belly

With white

Belly is worked flat.

R1: ch 6, turn, sc in 2nd ch from hook, sc 4 (5)

R2: ch 1, turn, inc, sc 3, inc (7)

R3: ch 1, turn, sc 7

R4: ch 1, turn, inc, sc 5, inc (9)

R5-7: ch 1, turn, sc 9

R8: ch 1, turn, dec, sc 5, dec (7)

R9: ch 1, turn, dec, sc 3, dec (5)

R10: ch 1, turn, dec, sc 1, dec (3)

Sc around entire belly.

FO, leave tail for sewing to body.

Sew to front of body.

Nose

With MC

R1: MR 6

R2: inc x6 (12)

R3: [inc, sc 1] x6 (18)

R4: [inc, sc 2] x6 (24)

R5-6: sc 24

R7: [dec, sc 2] x6 (18)

R8: sc 18

R9: [dec, sc 1] x6 (12)

R10: sc 12

FO, leave tail for sewing to face.

Stuff firmly.

Sew to face.

Tail

With MC

R1: MR 4

R2: [inc, sc 1] x2 (6)

R3: [inc, sc 2] x2 (8)

R4: [inc, sc 3] x2 (10)

R5: sc 2, inc, sc 4, inc, sc 2 (12)

R6: inc, hdc 5, inc, sc 5 (14)

R7: inc, hdc 6, inc, sc 6 (16)

R8: inc, hdc 7, inc, sc 7 (18)

FO, leave tail for sewing to body.

Stuff.

Sew to body.

Shell

With red

R1: MR 6

R2: [inc, sc 1] x3 (9)

R3: [inc, sc 2] x3 (12)

R4: sc 12

Change to white.

R5: Rev sc 12 (instructions below)

FO, leave tail for sewing to back.

Stuff lightly

Sew to back.

To reverse sc, you will work sc sts in the opposite direction you normally work
them. For example, if you are right handed and typically move to the left when
making your stitches, you instead work backwards and move to the right. It
makes a fun ridge design. Photos below, they are in a different color than what

you will be working with.

FO, weave in tail.

Arms – make 2

With MC

R1: MR 6

R2-8: sc 6

FO, leave tail for sewing to body.

Sew to sides of body.

No need to stuff arms.

Legs – make 2

With MC

R1: MR 6

R2: [inc, sc 1] x3 (9)

R3: [inc, sc 2] x3 (12)

R4: [inc, sc 3] x3 (15)

R5: sc 15

FO, leave tail for sewing to body.

Stuff lightly.

Sew to body.

Shoes – make 2

With CC1

R1: ch 4, turn, sc in in 2nd ch from hook, sc 1, 3 sc in next st, continue around to other side, sc 2, 2 sc in next st (9)

R2: inc, sc 2, inc x2, sc 3, inc (13)

Change to CC2

R3: BLO sc 13

R4: sc 13

R5: sc 4, hdc 5, sc 4 (13)

R6: sc 4, dec x2, sc 5 (11)

R7: sc 11

FO, leave tail for sewing to body.

Stuff

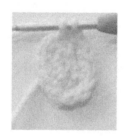

Sew to body. Shoes can be placed so they make Yoshi stand or sit.

Back Spikes – make 2

With red

[ch 4, turn, sl st in 2nd ch from hook, sc, hdc] x3

FO, leave tail

Sew 2 sets of back spikes together. This makes them firm so they won't curl.

Sew to back of head.

Congratulations!

Your Mini Gamer Friend is now complete and ready for play or display. I hope

you enjoyed making this pattern. I would love to see pictures of your finished
dolls!!
Note: Be careful when giving your finished plush to young ones. Your amigurumi
now contains small parts and pieces. If these pieces were to come off, they
could pose a choking hazard to small children and pets.

Koopa Troopa Pattern

Materials-

- Size G hook
- Yarn-Yellow, Cream, Green, Dark Green, White, and Light Brown
- Felt-White, Black, and Light Brown
- Yarn Needle
- Glue (optional)

Head-yellow

Rnd 1.Sc 6 in magic ring (6)

Rnd 2.Inc around (12)

Rnd 3.*Sc in next sc, Inc* around (18)

Rnd 4.*Sc in next 2 sc, Inc* around (24)

Rnd 5.*Sc in next 3 sc, Inc* around (30)

Rnd 6-8.Sc around

Rnd 9.*Sc in next 3 sc, Dec* around (24)

Rnd 10.*Sc in next 2 sc, Dec* around (18)

Rnd 11.*Sc in next sc, Dec* around (12)

Rnd 12.Dec around (6) F/O, stuff lightly, and close hole

Nose- yellow

Rnd 1.Sc 6 in magic ring (6)

Rnd 2.Inc around (12)

Rnd 3.*Sc in next sc, Inc* around (18)

Rnd 4.*Sc in next 2 sc, Inc* around (24)

Rnd 5-6.Sc around

Rnd 7.*Sc in next sc, Dec* around (16)

Rnd 8.*Sc in next 2 sc, Dec* around (12)

Rnd 9.Dec around (6) F/O, stuff, and close hole

Eyes-yellow (make 2)

Rnd 1.Sc 6 in magic ring (6)

Rnd 2.Inc around (12)

Rnd 3-7. Sc around, F/O and stuff

Neck-cream

Row 1.Ch 8, turn

Row 2.Sc in second ch from hook, sc across (7)

Rows 3-6.Ch1, turn, sc across

Roll up and sew

Shell-start with green

Rnd 1.Sc 6 in magic ring (6)

Rnd 2.Inc around (12)

Rnd 3.*Sc in next sc, Inc* around (18)

Rnd 4.*Sc in next 2 sc, Inc* around (24)

Rnd 5.*Sc in next 3 sc, Inc* around (30)

Rnd 6.*Sc in next 4 sc, Inc* around (36)

Rnd 7-8. Sc around, In last round, in last sc, switch to white

Rnd 9.FLO sc around

Rnd 10.Sc around

Rnd 11.BLO sc around, In last sc switch to cream

Rnd 12.FLO sc around

Rnd 13.*Sc in next 4 sc, Dec* around (30)

Rnd 14.*Sc in next 3 sc, Dec* around (24)

Rnd 15.*Sc in next 2 sc, Dec* around (18)

Rnd 16.*Sc in next sc, Dec* around (12)

Rnd 17.Dec around (6) F/O

Before you stuff- Sew together where the white ends and begins, matching up stitches. In the end there should be a white bump like in the picture.

Stuff and close hole

Arms-yellow (make 2)

Rnd 1.Sc 6 in magic ring (6)

Rnd 2.*Sc in next 2 sc, Inc* around (8)

Rnd 3-8.Sc around, Stuff

Flatten open side and match up stitches. Sc through both sides (4)

F/O

Sew together first and last sc to make a small circle

Legs-yellow (make 2)

Rnd 1.Sc 6 in magic ring (6)

Rnd 2.*Sc in next sc, Inc* around (9)

Rnd 3-8.Sc around

Dec once (8) Stuff

Flatten open side and match up stitches. Sc through both sides (4)

F/O

Shoes-green (make 2)

Rnd 1.Sc 6 in magic ring (6)

Rnd 2.Inc around (12)

Rnd 3.*Sc in next sc, Inc* around (18)

Rnd 4.BLO,*Sc 3 in one sc, sc in next 5 sc, sc 3 in one sc, sc in next 2 sc* twice (26)

Rnd 5.Sc around

Rnd 6.Dec around (13)

Rnd 7.Sc in next sc,*Sc in next 4 sc, Dec* around (11)

Rnd 8.FLO sc around

Rnd 9-11.Sc around F/O

Roll up top of Shoe and sew.

When you put the Leg in the Shoe some parts of the Shoe aren't stuffed. Stuff those parts.

Put Leg in Shoe. You don't have to sew it to secure it.

Tail-yellow

Rnd 1. Sc 6 in magic ring (6)

Rnd 2-3. Sc around

Assembly-

1. Cut out the eyes and bottom of shoes from felt
2. Sew or glue on felt to where it goes
3. With light brown, chain stitch stripes on belly of Shell and with dark green, chain stitch pattern on Shell
4. Sew on Neck to top part of Shell
5. Sew on Arms and Legs to Shell
6. Sew on Eyes and Nose to Head. Flatten top part of Head so Eyes won't pop out as much. (That's why I said stuff lightly)
7. Sew on Head to top part of Shell. (On top of Neck)
8. Sew on Tail to bottom back of Shell

Super Mario Crochet Design

Mario Bros. Cheep-Cheep

SIZE

Apprx. Height 5" and width from the widest point 6"

MATERIALS

*Crochet hook size 4mm

*Worsted weight yarn: Orange (57g), White (15g), Yellow (12g) and Beige (4g)

*Felt in small amounts: Black & White

*Yarn needle

*Fiberfill

PATTERN NOTES

Gauge isn't all that important, but your hook and yarn choices should result in a fairly tight stitch so that the stuffing won't show through.

Numbers in ( ) at the end of each round or row indicate the total number of stitches for that round or row.

BODY (starting with orange)

Rnd 1: 6 sc in Magic Ring (6)

Rnd 2: 2sc in each sc around (12)

Rnd 3: sc in next sc, 2sc in next sc around (18)

Rnd 4: sc in next 2sc, 2sc in next sc around (24)

Rnd 5: sc in next 3sc, 2sc in next sc around (30)

Rnd 6: sc in next 4sc, 2sc in next sc around (36)

Rnd 7: sc in next 5sc, 2sc in next sc around (42)

Rnd 8: sc in next 6sc, 2sc in next sc around (48)

Rnd 9: sc in next 19sc, in last sc change to white sc in next 10sc, in last sc change to orange sc in next 19 sc (48)

Rnd 10: *sc in next 7sc, 2sc in next sc* repeat from * to * 2times, sc in next 3sc, in last sc change to white sc in next 4sc, 2sc in next sc, sc in next 5sc, in last sc change to orange sc in next 2sc, 2sc in next sc, *sc in next 7sc, 2sc in next sc* repeat from * to * 2times (54)

Rnd 11-21: sc in next 21sc, in last sc change to white sc in next 11sc, in last sc change to orange sc in next 22sc (54)

Rnd 22: *sc in next 7sc, dec over next 2sc* repeat from * to * 2times, sc in next 3sc, in last sc change to white sc in next 4sc, dec over next 2sc, sc in next 5sc, in last sc change to orange sc in next

2sc, dec over next 2sc, *sc in next 7sc, dec over next 2sc* repeat from * to * 2times (48)

Rnd 23: sc in next 19sc, in last sc change to white sc in next 10sc, in last sc change to orange sc in next 19sc (48)

Rnd 24: *sc in next 6sc, dec over next 2sc* repeat from * to * 2times, sc in next 3sc, in last sc change to white sc in next 3sc, dec over next 2sc, sc in next 5sc, in last sc change to orange sc in next sc, dec over next 2sc, *sc in next 6sc, dec over next 2sc* repeat from * to * 2times (42)

Rnd 25: *sc in next 5sc, dec over next 2sc* repeat from * to * 2times, sc in next 3sc, in last sc change to white sc in next 2sc, dec over next 2sc, sc in next 5sc, in last sc change to orange dec over next 2sc, *sc in next 5sc, dec over next 2sc* repeat from * to * 2times (36)

Rnd 26: *sc in next 4sc, dec over next 2sc* repeat from * to * 2times, sc in next 3sc, in last sc change to white, sc in next sc, dec over next 2sc, sc in next 5sc, in last sc change to orange dec over next 2sc, sc in next 4sc, dec over next 2sc, sc in next 5sc (31)

Rnd 27: *sc in next 3sc, dec over next 2sc* repeat from * to * 2times, sc in next 3sc, in last sc change to white dec over next 2sc, sc in next 3sc, dec over next 2sc, in last sc change to orange *sc in next 3sc, dec over next 2sc* repeat from * to * 2times, sc in last sc (25)
Begin stuffing at this point if you haven't already. Stuff firmly while shaping as you go along.

Rnd 28: sc in next 11sc, in last sc change to white dec over next 2sc, sc in next sc, dec over next 2sc, in last sc change to orange sc in next 9sc (23)

Rnd 29: sc in next 11sc, in last sc change to white dec over all 3 white stitches, in last sc change to orange sc in next 9sc (21)

Rnd 30: *sc in next 2sc, dec over next 2sc* repeat from * to * 5times sc in last sc (16)

Rnd 31: *sc in next sc, dec over next 2sc* repeat from * to * 5times, sc in last sc (11)

Rnd 32: *dec over next 2sc* repeat from * to * 5timessc in last sc (6)

F/O, leave a tail for closing. Add any bits of stuffing needed to finish shaping the body nicely. Weave tail through the final row and draw up tight to close. Secure and weave in ends.

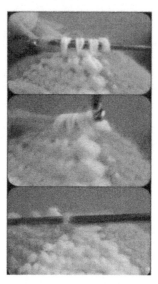

FIN (yellow)

Rnd 1: ch 8, skip 1st ch, *sc in next st, ch 2* repeat from * to * 4times, turn

Rnd 2: *sc, hdc, 2dc, hdc, sc* repeat in each ch2 loops, sl st in the end

F/O, weave in ends.

HAIR make 2 (yellow)

Rnd 1: ch 11, skip 1st ch,*2sc in next ch* repeat from * to * all the way around, ch3, turn (20)

Rnd 2: tr in next 4sc, dc in next 4sc, hdc in next 4sc, sc in next 8sc (20)

F/O, weave in ends.

On one of the hair pieces. The top part only & back loops only.

Rnd 1: ch 1, hdc in next 10 sts, sc in next 10sts, ch1 turn (20)

Rnd 2: Put together both of the hair piece and sl st on back loops only on top part and continue on to the side. F/O, weave in ends. Leave the bottom part open. sl st the other side. F/O, weave in ends. Stuff lightly.

Super Mario Crochet Design

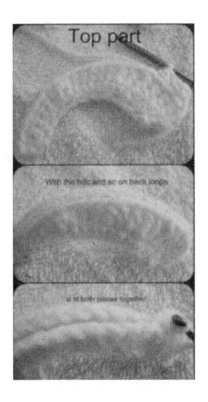

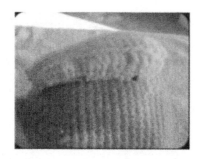

MOUTH (beige)

Rnd 1: 6 sc in Magic Ring (6)

Rnd 2: 2sc in each sc around (12)

Rnd 3: *sc in next 4sc, 2sc in next sc, 2sc in next sc* repeat from * to * 2times (16)

Rnd 4: back loops only for this round *sc in next 7sc, 2sc in next sc* repeat from * to * 2times (18)

Rnd 5: sc in each sc around (18)

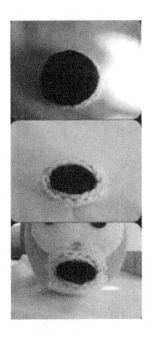

ASSEMBLY:

I highly recommend pinning all the pieces together before sewing anything to make sure you have all the pieces done right and that you get them in the positions you like best before sewing. It seems like alot of extra work, but this will save you ALOT of hassle.

As I have show you in the previous pictures. Place fin on the back just like shown in image 2.

Hair goes right on the middle of the top part. Align it right on the middle of the eyes.

Eyes are constructed from felt. See pictures for guidance on how to get your eyes to look like.

Mouth see image 5 for placement.

The fins that go on the side of Cheep-Cheep, I sketch them out first before drawing them in the felt.

Super Mario Crochet Design

Made in the USA
Monee, IL
26 October 2022